Seasons

by Robin Nelson

first step nonfiction

Lerner Publications · Minneapolis

Winter becomes spring.

Summer follows spring and turns into fall.

The **seasons** are a **cycle**.

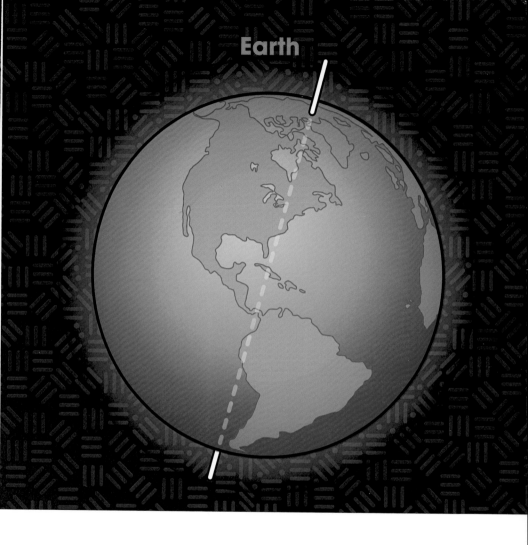

Earth

We have seasons because
Earth is **tilted**.

During cool seasons, Earth is tilted away from the Sun.

During warm seasons, Earth is tilted toward the Sun.

Winter brings the coldest
weather.

In winter, snow can cover
the ground.

In spring, the weather gets
warmer.

Every spring, plants grow
again.

Summer is the hottest season.

Every summer, the Sun shines
strongly.

In the fall, leaves change color.

Every fall, the weather gets cool.

After fall, winter comes
again.

Seasons change over and over every year.

Earth's Seasons

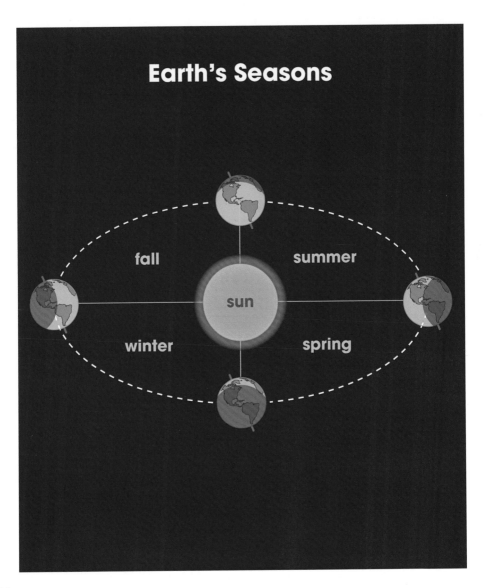

Learn More about the Seasons

Earth is tilted. At different times during the year, Earth's tilt puts some parts of Earth closer to the Sun's rays than other parts. When the top of Earth is tilted toward the Sun, the Sun's rays are stronger there. It is summer in that part of Earth. When the top of Earth is tilted away from the Sun, the Sun's rays are weaker. It is winter there.

Seasons Facts

 When it is summer on the top half of Earth, it is winter on the bottom half.

 At the North Pole and the South Pole, the Sun does not shine at all in the winter. It is dark all day. In the summer, the Sun shines all day and night.

 Near the middle of Earth, it is warm all year.

Some places in the world only have two seasons—a dry season and a rainy season.

 Storms with thunder and lightning happen more in the summer.

 Mount Baker, Washington, had the most snow in one winter. In the winter of 1998–1999, Mount Baker got 1,140 inches (2,895 centimeters) of snow.

Glossary

 cycle – something that happens over and over again over time

 Earth – the planet we live on

 seasons – four parts of the year

 tilted – tipped

Index

The images in this book are used with the permission of: © Tom Rosenthal/SuperStock, p. 2; © Luiz Felipe Castro/Flickr/Getty Images, pp. 3, 22 (second from bottom); © iStockphoto.com/ Philip Cooper, pp. 4, 22 (top); © Laura Westlund/Independent Picture Service, pp. 5, 18, 22 (second from top, bottom); © iStockphoto.com/Stephen Strathdee, p. 6; © iStockphoto.com/Xavi Arnau, p. 7; © Robert Daly/OJO Images/Getty Images, p. 8; © Jose Luis Pelaez/Iconica/Getty Images, p. 9; © Fancy/Alamy, p. 10; © Tobi Corney/Stone+/Getty Images, p. 11; © age fotostock/SuperStock, p. 12; © SuperStock RF/SuperStock, p. 13; © Dennis McColeman/ Photographer's Choice/Getty Images, p. 14; © Pfong001/Dreamstime.com, p. 15; © Thomas Barwick/Digital Vision/Getty Images, p. 16; © iStockphoto.com/Paul Tessier, p. 17.

Front Cover: © Matheisl/Taxi/Getty Images.

Lerner Publications Company
A division of Lerner Publishing Group, Inc.
241 First Avenue North
Minneapolis, MN 55401 USA

For reading levels and more information, look up this title at www.lernerbooks.com.

Library of Congress Cataloging-in-Publication Data

Nelson, Robin, 1971–
    Seasons / by Robin Nelson.
        p.   cm. — (First step nonfiction. Discovering nature's cycles)
    Includes index.
    ISBN 978–0–7613–4578–7 (lib. bdg. : alk. paper)
    ISBN 978–0–7613–6263–0 (EB pdf)
    1. Seasons—Juvenile literature. 2. Earth—Orbit—Juvenile literature. I. Title.
QB637.4.N45 2011
508.2—dc22   20090206113

Manufactured in the United States of America
3 - 38762 - 10534 - 5/11/2016

Also available as a Lerner Interactive Book™

Lerner DIGITAL

Discovering Nature's Cycles

Day and Night

Earth's Water Cycle

Hibernation

Migration

The Night Sky

Seasons

First Step Nonfiction

ISBN 978-0-7613-5684-4

90000

9 780761 356844

LernerClassroom™
A division of Lerner Publishing Group
www.lernerbooks.com
005–008 Lexile: 480 Guided Reading: H